NEW VANGUARD • 141

SHERMAN FIREFLY

DAVID FLETCHER   ILLUSTRATED BY TONY BRYAN

First published in Great Britain in 2008 by Osprey Publishing,
Midland House, West Way, Botley, Oxford OX2 0PH, UK
443 Park Avenue South, New York, NY 10016, USA
E-mail: info@ospreypublishing.com

A CIP catalogue record for this book is available from the British Library

ISBN: 978 1 84603 277 6

Page layout by Melissa Orrom Swan, Oxford
Index by Joan Dearnley
Typeset in Sabon and Myriad Pro
Originated by United Graphic Pte Ltd., Singapore
Printed in China through World Print Ltd

09 10 11 12 13   12 11 10 9 8 7 6 5 4 3

FOR A CATALOGUE OF ALL BOOKS PUBLISHED BY OSPREY
PLEASE CONTACT:

NORTH AMERICA
Osprey Direct, c/o Random House Distribution Center, 400 Hahn Road,
Westminster, MD 21157
E-mail: uscustomerservice@ospreypublishing.com

ALL OTHER REGIONS
Osprey Direct, The Book Service Ltd, Distribution Centre, Colchester Road, Frating Green,
Colchester, Essex, CO7 7DW
E-mail: customerservice@ospreypublishing.com

Osprey Publishing is supporting the Woodland Trust, the UK's leading
woodland conservation charity, by funding the dedication of trees.

www.ospreypublishing.com

EDITOR'S NOTE

For ease of comparison between types, imperial measurements are used
almost exclusively throughout this book. The exception is weapon calibres,
which are given in their official designation, whether metric or imperial. The
following data will help in converting the imperial measurements to metric:

1 mile = 1.6km
1lb = 0.45kg
1 yard = 0.9m
1ft = 0.3m
1in. = 2.54cm/25.4mm
1 gal = 4.5 liters
1 ton (US) = 0.9 tonnes
1hp = 0.745kW

AUTHOR'S NOTE

The author wishes to thank Richard C. Harley.

All images contained in this book are kindly provided by The Tank Museum,
Bovington.

CONTENTS

INTRODUCTION   4

THE 17-POUNDER   5

DEVELOPMENTS AT LULWORTH   9

DESIGNING THE FIREFLY   13

THE CONVERSION PROGRAMME   24

AMMUNITION   28

CONCRETE BUSTERS   32

THE FIREFLY IN ACTION   36

THE AMERICAN ANGLE   43

SUPPLY AND DEMAND   45

WHAT'S IN A NAME?   46

INDEX   48

SHERMAN FIREFLY

INTRODUCTION

Anyone who studies tank history is, in the end, bound to conclude that the most important feature of any tank is its gun. True, there are other factors. If you're a member of the crew, then protection comes high on the list. Those who conduct battles would favour excellent mobility, while others will be heard demanding greater reliability, improved communications, or longer range. All of these things are important. But when it comes down to it, the gun is what it is all about, and that gun, in the majority of cases, is required to be particularly good at destroying other tanks.

There are reasons why British tank armament failed to keep pace in the early years of World War II. Some of them are justifiable, but the majority are not. In summer 1940, following the dramatic events culminating in the fall of France, MajGen Vyvyan Pope told the War Office that the next generation of tanks would need more powerful guns. The trouble was that the next generation of tanks, particularly the Crusader, had already been designed around the existing 2-pounder gun (see New Vanguard 14: *Crusader and Covenanter Cruiser Tanks 1939–45*), and nobody seems to have considered making arrangements for improving things if and when a new gun became available.

31 August 1944: a Firefly of Guards Armoured Division crossing the railway at Beaurains. A good deal of foliage, held in place by a net, has been draped over the hull with similar applications over the turret and gun. Spare track links appear on the front of the hull and sides of the turret, but most obvious of all is the Prong device at the front, a variation on Sgt Culin's inspired design. All are suggestive of service in the Bocage country.

That had to wait until a further generation of tanks, typified by the Cromwell, appeared (see New Vanguard 104: *Cromwell Cruiser Tank 1942–50*), but this took so long to happen that the tank was already out of date when it entered service, and once again, the designers had failed to build in the ability to improve, should a better weapon appear. Of course, the Cromwell was a special case. Its introduction had been delayed by the need to replace tanks lost in France, and the same was true of its gun, the 57mm 6-pounder. British practice, since the advent of the 2-pounder, was to design a gun to fit a field carriage, and once that was in production, to alter the gun to suit a tank mounting.

Yet production of the 6-pounder was in arrears while the Army's lost stock of 2-pounder anti-tank guns was replaced. As a result, although the new cruiser tank, the Cromwell, was designed to take the 6-pounder, by the time it was considered fit for service, the priority had changed. The dedicated anti-tank gun was out of favour for tanks, and in any case, with regular ammunition, the 6-pounder was effectively out of date. Thus, no Cromwell tank ever actually went into action with the 6-pounder, which for other reasons, was something of a pity.

Lulworth was undoubtedly the spiritual home of the Firefly, and this VC sports the cannon insignia of the Royal Armoured Corps Gunnery School. It is an early conversion, fitted with brackets for the Houseboat disguise. Note also the patch of armour used to seal off the redundant hull machine gun aperture.

THE 17-POUNDER

The Ministry of Information film *A Date with a Tank*, released in 1944, offered a dramatic portrayal of the design and construction of the first batch of 17-pounder anti-tank guns against a deadline to have some of them in the field before the rumoured German heavy tank, the Pz Kpfw VI Tiger, put in an appearance. There was an element of truth in this, although the timescale was shortened for dramatic effect.

Thinking in the Royal Artillery was far ahead of those responsible for designing British tanks. This is illustrated by the fact that the very first requirement for an anti-tank gun of about a 3-in. calibre, firing a projectile weighing about 17lb, was being considered as early as 21 November 1940. That was a year before the first 6-pounder anti-tank gun – the weapon it was due to supersede – entered production.

In the meantime, just to confuse the issue, British tank and gun designers had been led away from the true path by unfortunate experience and heretical foreign practice. The experience was Gen Erwin Rommel's habit of intermingling tanks and anti-tank guns, and the latter, being small and inconspicuous, were difficult targets for a gun that only fired a small calibre round of solid shot. The heresy, which came as a package with successive American medium tank designs, was the belief that tanks should be a form of mobile artillery to support the infantry first and secondly, an anti-tank gun, since that role, according to American doctrine, was reserved for something that looked like a tank but wasn't a tank, known optimistically as a Tank Destroyer. Thus an American tank gun of this period was a dual-purpose

1. SHERMAN VC FIREFLY, 21ST ARMOURED REGIMENT, 4TH CANADIAN ARMOURED BRIGADE, 4TH CANADIAN ARMOURED DIVISION, NOVEMBER 1944

The idea that adding surplus track links to your tank could improve the armour protection seems to be universal. It could be found applied to British tanks in Gaza in 1917 and on Challenger tanks in the Gulf in 1991; but it reached a high point in World War II, most particularly among Canadian armoured regiments who in effect covered their Shermans with whatever type of track they could find. A British officer who studied the phenomenon at the time pronounced it totally ineffective. All it did, in his view, was to increase the weight of the tank to an unacceptable level. However, he also recognized that it was a symptom of the crews' lack of confidence in the armour of their tanks. Indeed, he said, crews had firm beliefs in how these track links should be arranged and attached. Some believed that the tracks should be fixed with the outer surface outwards; others insisted that the inner surface should face outwards so that incoming rounds might be deflected by raised portions. Then there were those who welded the tracks to the hull, while others recommended that they should hang loose and absorb some of the impact. Whatever the system, the tracks added a fair amount of weight to a tank that was already overloaded, but they seem to have survived. Markings, of course, were totally obscured.

Under the Canadian system armoured regiments were simply numbered, but all had fine traditional titles; 21st Armoured Regiment was the prosaic alternative for the Governor General's Foot Guards. In October and November 1944 they were in action east of Bruges, up to the Scheldt estuary.

2. SHERMAN IC FIREFLY WITH TULIP ROCKETS, C SQUADRON, 1ST COLDSTREAM GUARDS, GUARDS ARMOURED DIVISION, NEAR BREMEN, 12 APRIL 1945

During the fighting in the Rhineland, over the winter of 1944–45, 1st Battalion The Coldstream Guards acquired some rockets and launching rails normally fitted beneath the wings of Hawker Typhoon fighters for use in the ground attack role. Not having enough to equip the entire regiment, the regimental fitters were told to fit them to the tanks of C Squadron, Fireflies and regular Shermans alike.

It was a peculiar thing to do. The rockets with their 60lb warhead were devastating enough but, even when fired from a diving aircraft, were not renowned for their precision or accuracy. Launched from a tank, which had to halt in order to fire, they were wildly inaccurate but most spectacular. In our drawing one of C Squadron's Fireflies has just fired a Tulip, as the rockets were called, and awaits the result. The rockets were suspended from launching rails on either side of the turret, aimed using the tank commander's sighting vane and then fired electrically. With no other velocity behind it the rocket first dips, then picks up speed and races away in the general direction of the target. There is no evidence that a rocket was ever fired at a German AFV, which it probably would not have hit in any case – if it had the results might have been quite impressive.

The missiles were usually used against manned road blocks or woods where enemy troops might be hiding and the effect was salutary. Road blocks were simply blown away, while anyone who thought they were safe in a wood invariably changed their minds and surrendered after they had experienced a rocket or two from the receiving end. Whether the attachments were ever worth the trouble of fitting, the risks of carrying them is another matter altogether.

1

2

An official photo of another early VC conversion that also has the Houseboat brackets. Compared with the prototype, viewed from more or less the same angle, note the support for the open loader's hatch, the access panels on top of the radio box, and the barrel support in the centre of the rear deck.

weapon capable of firing both high explosive and armour-piercing ammunition. It was pounced upon with delight by British tank crews as an antidote to Rommel's anti-tank gun menace, and for a while at least, something that could match German armour in a tank-versus-tank fight. Yet the Germans were soon ahead of the game once more. In summer 1942, they introduced an improved version of the Panzer IV with a long, high-velocity anti-tank gun that opened up fighting ranges even more and placed the British at a disadvantage yet again. It is probably worth remarking at this stage that German schemes to up-gun their existing tanks not only did so without affecting the tank's general performance, but they also involved improvements in armour protection.

Clearly, as far as the British were concerned, the time had come to adopt the 17-pounder as a tank gun, although at this time no suitable tank was available. Whose fault was that? Historically, since about 1943, the British have been castigated for their failure to match the Germans in the design of heavy, big-gun tanks. It is only fair to point out that at a Tank Board meeting held in London on 9 December 1941, the idea was discussed of fitting the new 17-pounder into a tank. It has been suggested that this is associated with General Staff specification A29 calling for a 45-ton tank – a large cruiser – with a 17-pounder armament and what are described rather vaguely as 'twin tracks'. This was to be a Rolls-Royce project, which may well be so, but proof is lacking. What we do know is that A29 was dropped in favour of another 17-pounder design, based upon the Cromwell and known as A30 and that work on this tank got under way in 1942. Tanks do not spring out of the ground fully formed, nor grow on trees, and even under the pressures of war there is a long period between the idea of a tank being mooted and its ultimate appearance. This may well explain the preference for A30, which was largely a modification to an existing design, rather than something entirely new.

Even so, the progress of A30 from concept to finished article was long and wearisome. In the meantime, the Tank Board and the General Staff laid down specifications for two more 17-pounder tanks, the short-term A34, later to

become the Comet, and the long-term A41, the future Centurion. Both were proposed in summer 1943, and both would turn out to be excellent tanks of their kind. Yet the former would only be ready in time to see a few weeks' service before the war with Germany ended and the latter just too late to take part at all. What mattered to the Allied tank men was the here and now.

7 June 1944: a Firefly and other Shermans of A Squadron 3rd County of London Yeomanry form up after landing on D plus one, inland from their landing point at Mont Fleury. The Firefly in the foreground has a stowage box across the front, a camouflage net on the turret, and a muzzle cover on the end of the gun.

DEVELOPMENTS AT LULWORTH

The credit for initiating the design of what became the Sherman Firefly should probably go to a Royal Tank Regiment major named George Brighty who in 1943 was based at the Royal Armoured Corps Gunnery School at Lulworth in Dorset. Despite the fact that A30, the official Challenger in name and practice, was already undergoing initial gunnery trials at Lulworth, Brighty seems to have been convinced that the Sherman was a better mount for the 17-pounder. But he was stymied by the turret, which was too small and cramped to accept the big gun, and in particular, the substantial recoil system that would be required in a tank. Brighty was almost certainly working on an unofficial basis, and it would be interesting to know how he got hold of a tank, particularly one he intended to butcher in order to prove his case.

This was the stage Brighty had reached when he was joined by an old colleague, another Royal Tank Regiment major named George Witheridge who, as it happened, was also bent on improving the firepower of the Sherman. The difference was that Witheridge had experienced the inadequacy of the firepower of British and American tanks first hand. He was in the Western Desert in Africa, commanding C Squadron of 3rd RTR, when he was blown out of his Grant at the battle of Gazala in May 1942. It was probably no accident that the first Grant tanks to arrive in the Middle East went to 3rd RTR if George Witheridge was with the regiment. The Grant was the tank that first expanded the British experience of tank gunnery, in particular the use of high explosive rounds, which Witheridge seems to have been concerned with at this time.

Although he recovered from his wounds, George Witheridge was not considered fit to return to combat duty. So, based upon his pre-war experience with experimental gunnery at Lulworth, Witheridge soon found himself appointed to the Middle East Gunnery School in Egypt. While there he met Gen Jacob Devers, probably one of the most underrated American armour officers. Devers must have been impressed because he invited Witheridge to spend some time at Fort Knox, Kentucky, to advise on tank gunnery techniques. The British officer's experience of American tanks in combat would also be seen as a strong recommendation. George Witheridge arrived at Knox on a six-month posting in January 1943.

In June 1943, George Witheridge returned to Lulworth, clearly sold on the value of American tanks, and in particular, the Sherman. For a year or more before the Grant arrived, British tank crews had been crying out for a tank gun that could fire both armour-piercing and high-explosive rounds. While he was in Egypt, we know that Witheridge was concerning himself primarily with the development of high explosive ammunition, and this can only have been reinforced by his time at Fort Knox, where the creed saw the tank more as an infantry support than an anti-tank weapon. The difference was that Witheridge was also concerned with improving the armour-piercing firepower of British tanks while retaining the ability to fire high explosive rounds. Witheridge tells us that after his stint at Fort Knox, he expected to go back to Egypt. Therefore his posting to Lulworth came as something of a surprise.

In January 1943, while Witheridge was in the United States, the Chief Inspector of Gunnery at Lulworth had many unkind things to say about the A30 Challenger; not specifically on the design, which was poor, but on the concept of a tank that was clearly designed to fight against other tanks to the virtual exclusion of anything else. This was the old British doctrine, and it had clearly been replaced, in many minds, by the American idea of the tank as a multi-purpose weapon. The trouble is, of course, that if anti-tank supremacy had to be sacrificed to achieve this, then there was clearly something wrong.

There are indeed a number of things that did not add up. One practical objection to the A30 Challenger that was raised at Lulworth concerned armour thickness. This had been sacrificed as a concession to weight in order to accommodate the larger gun and turret, even to the point where A30 was less well protected than the Cromwell from which it was derived. The Lulworth view on this was that a tank designed to fight other tanks, which of course A30 was, should also be well armoured so that it might survive a stand-up fight. But if that was to be the doctrine, why was George Brighty permitted to carry on with his work on the Sherman?

Not that Brighty was having an easy time of it. The 17-pounder would fit into the turret, but it seemed to be impossible, within the confined space available, to contain the recoil. The force was simply too great. There was a solution, but it had probably never been tried in a tank. This was to lock the gun firmly into the turret so that the recoil effect was absorbed by the mass of the tank and the cushioning effect of its suspension. Brighty tried it and it worked, but there was no telling how long a tank would last under such treatment.

This was the state of affairs when George Witheridge arrived. He inspected the A30 Challenger and joined the chorus of complaints about its design. Then he looked at what Brighty was up to and became distinctly nervous. This rigid gun mounting seemed to break all the rules. When he first test-fired it, Witheridge remained outside the turret and tugged on a lanyard. Having fired off three rounds this way, Witheridge saw nothing awful happening and climbed into the turret to fire seven more rounds. Even so, his advice to Brighty, for the benefit of future tank crews, was to continue work on developing a recoil system.

Whether the arrival of Witheridge at Lulworth attracted attention to Brighty's project or whether it was already known we cannot say, but it seems that not long after the former's arrival, a directive came down from the Department of Tank Design (DTD) that work on the up-gunned Sherman must cease. Again, it is difficult to say whether this was decided on technical grounds or because it might threaten the DTD's own project – A30. We may never know; maybe it was a bit of each.

Either way, this was not acceptable to George Witheridge. Possibly, he had been bitten by the bug because he was now clearly a convert to the idea

16 July 1944: a classic view of a 1st Northamptonshire Yeomanry Firefly in the Odon Valley, west of Caen. The Firefly is a IC fitted with the T62 type ribbed-metal track design. The British had a poor opinion of the alternative rubber block track.

8 August 1944: battle debut of the 1st Polish Armoured Division. A long line of Shermans, with a Firefly in the foreground, prepare to play their part in the attack towards Falaise. The Poles were organized and administered as part of the British Army, so the number 51 indicates the senior regiment – 1st Polish Armoured Regiment – in 10th Polish Armoured Brigade.

of a 17-pounder Sherman, and unlike Brighty, he had friends in high places. MajGen Raymond Briggs, like George Witheridge and Brighty, was a Royal Tank Regiment officer, which counts for a lot, but he and Witheridge were also old desert hands (Briggs had commanded the 1st Armoured Division). In August 1943, Raymond Briggs was appointed Director Royal Armoured Corps (DRAC), and it seems that he approved of what was going on at Lulworth. Like Witheridge, Briggs was a firm advocate of good tank gunnery, and in particular, he was keen to open up fighting ranges, which had been a serious problem for British tanks in the desert, in the face of long-range anti-tank guns.

To be fair, Briggs was not solely concerned with anti-tank fighting. Like Witheridge, he was also keen to develop what are known as indirect fire techniques, where the tanks act more like artillery, firing at targets they cannot actually see. This is normally associated with the use of high-explosive rounds, not armour piercing. On the other hand, work was heading in the right direction, and Briggs may have seen an opportunity to further his cause this way. After all, although it was primarily an anti-tank gun, the 17-pounder could fire a respectable high explosive shell out to a range of 10,000yds, and that must have appealed to Raymond Briggs.

Lacking the authority to set the ball rolling, Briggs put his case to Claude Gibb, the Director General of Weapon and Instrument Production at the Ministry of Supply, and gained his approval. As a result, however, the project was effectively taken out of the hands of the people at Lulworth and placed on an altogether more official footing. The days of the enthusiastic, gifted amateur were over. From now on, the professionals would move in.

8 August 1944: a VC of 8th Armoured Brigade, probably 24th Lancers, near St Leger on the Bayeux–Caen road. Both turret hatches are open, but the crew are keeping their heads down so they may be anticipating action.

DESIGNING THE FIREFLY

In fact, there was just one professional assigned to the project, a Mr W. G. K. Kilbourn, who at the time was assigned to the Department of Tank Design at Chertsey, although in normal times he was a professional engineer employed by Vickers. Not a great deal is known about him, but he must have been a gifted engineer because he tackled and solved the problems that had baffled Brighty; and indeed did it in an ingenious way.

In its regular role as an anti-tank gun, the 17-pounder employed a hydropneumatic recoil system with a travel of 40in., which was far too long for the cramped interior of a Sherman turret. Kilbourn therefore decided to replace the existing recoil cylinders with shorter ones. They would be mounted either side of the gun tube, but above and below the centre line of the barrel on opposite sides, all in a special cradle. So far so good, but despite the shorter recoil movement, Kilbourn noticed that the barrel tube was not as well supported as it was on the towed gun because the cradle which he had designed, although totally surrounding the barrel, had inevitably been shortened in order to fit into the turret. The remedy for this was to increase the contact between the barrel and the cradle, and since it was patently impossible to lengthen the cradle, this would mean modifying the barrel tube.

Artillerymen and gun makers have a vocabulary all their own, calling that part of a gun barrel that tapers forwards from the breech the 'chase'. Kilbourn reckoned that in order to improve contact with the cradle, it was necessary to extend the gun tube at a constant diameter, and in effect, move the chase further forward. This was a major engineering task: a sleeve had to be added to the barrel and then turned on a large lathe to produce the desired result.

If Kilbourn thought that he had solved the problem with these modifications to the gun he was wrong. The ingenuity he had employed to fit the weapon into the tank was commendable, but there were other matters to consider, in particular the crew and the ammunition. The big gun, with a strong recoil guard behind the breech, virtually divided the turret into two halves. This meant that the loader, on the left side of the gun, would find it very difficult to escape in a hurry if the tank were to be hit and brew up.

August 1944: a Sherman VC (M4A4) Firefly of Guards Armoured Division on the way east. The 'tracks' are taking a cross-country route to leave the roads free for wheeled transport. By this time, a number of regiments seem to have devised simple devices to support the gun in a forward position. This one also retains support brackets for the Houseboat disguise, although it never appears to have been used.

It would mean wriggling under the gun, climbing onto the commander's seat, and then sliding out through his hatch. The solution was to create a hatch for the loader on the left side, which had another advantage: it made it a lot easier to pass the larger rounds that were required for the big gun into the turret for stowage.

And that was not all. When the US Army adopted the Sherman tank, following the appearance of the prototype T6 in September 1941, they also adopted the British practice of fitting the radio set in the rear of the turret rather than in the hull. The Americans used their SCR 508 set, which was somewhat larger than its British equivalent, although mounting brackets were provided for both. The British No.19 set, linked with the smaller No.38 set, was perched at the back of the turret where the loader, who doubled as wireless operator, could reach to manipulate the controls. Whether, as some say, a set in this position would actually be destroyed by the recoil movement of the 17-pounder is open to doubt, but it must have come too close for comfort and certainly too close for the loader to operate it properly.

The solution, which may or may not have been devised by Kilbourn, was to cut a hole in the armour at the back of the turret and then weld on an armoured box, large enough to contain the radios that were dropped in from above and then covered with a lid. It has to be said that the opening in the armour was hardly a work of art. In the preserved Firefly at the Tank Museum in Bovington, Dorset, it is a relatively small hole, very roughly cut,

B

1. SHERMAN VC FIREFLY *BEUTE-PANZER*

It is not entirely clear how many Fireflies fell into German hands in serviceable condition. At least four have been identified from photographs, all M4A4 VC, and of these one is known to have come from 4th County of London Yeomanry at Villers-Bocage. Another appears to have been Canadian.

Whether any of them saw combat in the hands of their new owners is unclear but the number would be limited due to the lack of ammunition. It seems more likely that, if they were used at all it would have been as decoys or stalking horses. The tank represented here appears to have been used mainly for evaluation, familiarization and recognition purposes.

With surviving black-and-white photographs as the only source of information it would be unwise to attempt any definitive statements about camouflage colours although it is probably safe to say that they would not be as exotic as some representations suggest. On the other hand our subject shows no evidence of British markings so it may well have been over-painted. Photographs show it being tested and examined by German troops and with the eye of faith it is possible to discern patches that could be different colours. However, apart from the German crosses, this artwork only represents one interpretation.

2. SHERMAN VC FIREFLY, 2ND BATTALION IRISH GUARDS, GUARDS ARMOURED DIVISION, NETHERLANDS 1944

2nd Irish Guards' VC Firefly, copied from a snapshot taken by a local inhabitant during the liberation of the Netherlands. Many people have chalked slogans or their names onto the hull of the tank but the crew have gone one better and in bold letters written GEEN CIGARETTE on the side to discourage the locals from asking.

The tank is entirely standard but there are some interesting details. Brackets holding jerrycans are fitted to each side of the turret radio box, and patches of appliqué armour have been welded to the side of the hull including the so-called 'cheek' pieces on the front quarters of the turret. They added 1in. to the armour in these areas although they did not, on the hull at least, exactly match the ammunition stowage arrangements of the Firefly, having been designed for the regular 75mm gun tank.

Notice too that the second and third suspension units on this side feature the earlier, spoked-pattern road wheels.

A Firefly prototype or mock-up photographed at Chertsey. The gun may not be real, but a loader's hatch has been installed in the turret roof and the armoured container for the radios fitted at the rear, the lid for which is lying on the engine deck. The tank is an M4A4, or Sherman V, presumably the one that Kilbourn was working on.

through which the loader had to reach in order to manipulate the knobs. That box, such an obvious protrusion on the back of the turret, is probably the best way of identifying a Sherman Firefly if you cannot see the gun.

The ammunition supplied for the 17-pounder was naturally larger and heavier than any previously carried in a British tank. Therefore it was particularly difficult to manage in the confines of a Sherman turret that it had not been designed to fit. An average round was 32.8in. long (projectile and case together) and weighed 35.5lb. Even those rounds stowed within easy reach of the loader would have been difficult to load if the gun was mounted in the conventional way – with a vertical-acting breech block – because there was a risk of the cartridge case catching on something at the back of the turret before the pointed end of the projectile was properly lined up with the breech. One only has to imagine how awkward this could be in the middle of a tense action to realize that some improvement would be highly desirable.

The answer, and this is something we must attribute to Kilbourn, was to redesign the breech ring so that the block moved sideways, rather than up and down, which in turn meant that the loader did not need to raise the round so high and could load it with a turning motion. This brings up another point that might not be obvious at first. In British tanks, at least since the start of World War II, the commander had been located on the left side of the turret, with the gunner in front of him and the loader on the right. These positions were reversed on the Sherman and most American tanks, so it was vital that the open side of the breech ring lay to the left.

That it was not simply a matter of turning the gun on its side may be seen from photographs where, among other things, the breech closing spring case has been relocated to the right side. In this form, the gun was designated 17-pounder, quick-firing Mark IV, quick-firing indicating that it used one-piece ammunition. The plant selected to manufacture the new gun was the Royal Ordnance Factory, known locally as Barnbow, near Leeds. There had been a shell-filling factory at Barnbow in World War I, but this had been knocked down between the wars, and the site taken over by a coal mine. The new factory – officially Royal Ordnance Factory No.9 – had been built about a mile from the original site in 1939, and it was equipped to produce gun barrels.

This was all fairly conventional work since the guns were established types for which proper working drawings were available. The Mark IV 17-pounder was another matter. It was an urgent requirement, and when work began on the first two guns, the final assembly drawings were still being produced. It is difficult to date the period of Kilbourn's work except to say that it must have been from about August to early November 1943. The design team at Barnbow are a bit more specific in this respect. They tell us that the first drawings for what they called the 'SH-SH' gun were ready on 11 November 1943, and the first weapon was completed and issued to the Chief Inspector of Artillery on the 28th, followed two days later by the second gun. They were so proud of this that they lined up behind what was, presumably, the second gun and had themselves photographed for posterity. The prototype guns were successfully proof tested at Woolwich and Shoeburyness, clearing the way for production to commence.

1 September 1944: other elements of Guards Armoured Division reach Fouilly on the Somme. Here a standard 75mm Sherman is followed by a Firefly and what appears to be a turretless Stuart. The buildings in the background are French memorials to victims of the Somme fighting of 1916.

These four gentlemen, we must suppose, are the individuals who produced the redesigned 17-pounder. Features to note are the reshaped rear end of the barrel, the sideways-operating breech block, and the new location of the spring case – low down on the near side of the breech ring.

22 September 1944: a partially camouflaged VC Firefly of the Irish Guards with a column of Shermans crossing the bridge at Nijmegen during the attempt to relieve Arnhem. Netting covers the hull front and turret of the Firefly, which also has vegetation attached to the gun tube, although it looks a bit incongruous here.

Returning to ammunition, and by way of comparison, it should be noted that a typical 75mm round for a Sherman tank was about 26in. long, 6in. shorter than a 17-pounder round. Inevitably, it would mean that the ammunition stowage inside the Firefly would have to be rearranged to accommodate the new rounds. A regular 75mm gun M4A4 (Sherman V) had stowage for 97 main armament rounds, whereas the 17-pounder variant had racks to stow 78 rounds (although for practical reasons only 77 rounds would be carried).

Yet it was not simply a question of opening up the tank and stacking the rounds in wherever they would fit. Regular stowage arrangements had to be worked out that suited the tank and the location of the loader, not to mention the physical difficulties faced by the loader in handling the ammunition and getting it to the gun. The arrangement of stowage within a Sherman VC Firefly was eventually developed – in the turret itself were two small bins containing two and three rounds respectively. These were easy for the loader to access, and a skilled man could load them at the rate of six or seven seconds per round. Once they were used up, the loader turned to another bin, at his feet, which contained a further 18 rounds. In fact, the container had space for 20 rounds but two would be blocked by the gun mounting and could not be used. These rounds were stowed point-downwards at an angle of 40 degrees, pointing forwards. Once the turret floor plates that covered

18 October 1944: 11th Armoured Division, probably 3rd RTR, east of Venray, with infantry aboard. A Firefly with some additional track across the front at the head of a troop of Shermans on a typically muddy road. The 17-pounder is unmasked, and there is a .30in. Browning machine gun on the commander's cupola.

them had been removed, the rounds could be grasped by the base and dragged up onto the loader's lap – he was encouraged to sit when loading from this bin. Here he removed the protective clip from the base of the cartridge case and offered the round up to the breech of the gun. This motion took about nine or ten seconds. The only limitation when drawing rounds from this bin was the position of the turret relative to the ammunition stowage. As the turret turned, the floor panels covered the rounds, limiting those that the loader could reach. However, it was generally assumed that the tank's gun would be aimed across a relatively narrow frontal arc, so this problem was not regarded as serious. The chances of a Firefly in action having to traverse its turret more than a few degrees either side of 12 o'clock, let alone turn even further around – over its shoulder, as it were – did not appear to be very likely and could be discounted. To clarify this, if the main armament was pointing straight ahead in the at 12 o'clock position, then this 18-round bin could be reached with the gun pointing anywhere from 10 o'clock on the left side to 3 o'clock on the right.

August 1944: tiresome work on a warm summer day. A crew of C Squadron, 1st Northants Yeomanry top up the ammunition in their Firefly. It is going in through the redundant hull machine gunner's hatch and must be handled with the greatest care.

Even so, we have not yet accounted for the bulk of the ammunition, all of which was much harder to get at. Forty rounds were stowed in a pair of bins beneath the turret floor on the right side, where the loader was never going to be able to reach them in normal combat conditions. To make matters worse, the rounds were stowed horizontally, in five layers of four rounds, so that they had to be gripped and lifted bodily upwards. As if this were not enough, this ammunition could only be removed from these bins when the turret was in a specific position. In the case of the foremost bin, the turret had to be turned to a point midway between four and five o'clock and then farther round to somewhere near eight o'clock to uncover the rear bin. These bins were therefore regarded as inaccessible in combat and were referred to as replenishment bins. All of which meant that under average circumstances, the gunner of a Firefly had just 23 rounds available to him, after which there would be a pause while the turret crew replenished the ready rounds.

We are left with just 15 more rounds to account for, at least in theory, and these are the cause of the final, rather more drastic, alteration to the basic Sherman. The bin for these 15 rounds was situated to the right of the driver, on the opposite side of the transmission, where the hull machine gunner would normally be situated. Since there was no one to fire it, the machine gun and its mounting were removed and a bevel-edged segment of armour welded over the aperture. This is another very obvious indication, if nothing else can be seen, that the tank in question is, or was, a Firefly.

However, if the two 20-round bins under the turret floor were difficult to access, this one was downright impossible. The rounds were stowed vertically, point upwards, which made them extremely difficult to get a decent grip on. To make matters worse, one location, at the back of the bin, was so

difficult to get at, that it was not used, reducing the rounds available to 14. Furthermore, the five rearmost rounds were so difficult to remove and pass back into the turret that the normal drill – done only when the tank was out of action – was to pass them up through the absent hull machine gunner's hatch and then in through the loader's hatch. It was a task that involved at least three of the crew. This could be done with all 14 rounds although it was soon learned that with a bit of effort and contortion, the driver could reach over and pass back the nine rounds at the front of the bin into the turret without having to lift them outside the tank. Of course, this was only possible when the driver had nothing else to do.

If the processes outlined above seem to be organized and thoroughly worked out, it is probably true to say that this was more by accident than design. Although crews were instructed in the use of these new tanks before they went to war, this would have been done on just the barest minimum of experience, and it seems highly likely that the details were worked out by individual regiments in the field. Any effort to standardize and formalize the

December 1944: Lieutenant Boscawen's IC Hybrid of the 1st Coldstream Guards on the banks of the Meuse, acting as a backstop in the event of a German breakthrough. Camouflage netting appears to have been used on the rocket launchers on each side of the turret as well as on the turret itself, but it is a bit thin on the hull. Extended end connectors are fitted to the outside edge of each track.

practice had to wait until the end of the war. In July 1945, the Army Operational Research Group reported on a trial that it had run at Lulworth on stowage and loading of the 17-pounder gun in the Sherman VC. It seemed a strange time to do it, with the war over and the Sherman Firefly destined, as we know now, never to fire a shot in anger again in British service.

To round off the matter of turret armament, the gun mounting included a separate cradle, attached to the left side of the main cradle, which contained an M1919 Browning .30-in. machine gun, lined up to operate co-axially with the main gun. Both the 17-pounder and the Browning were fired electrically. Two buttons on the turret floor, within easy reach of the gunner's foot, enabled him to fire the machine gun by pressing down on the left button or fire the main armament by putting his boot on the right button. This last, however, was protected by a safety switch so that the mechanism would not operate during the loading process.

To the right of the main gun was another cradle that supported the gunner's sighting telescope, the No.43, x3 L, Mk I, which was calibrated for the 17-pounder and the machine gun. The gunner also had a pivoting periscope in the turret roof that was linked to the gun itself so that it moved through the same arc of elevation (plus 25 to minus 5 degrees) as the main weapon. Finally, the turret also contained a 2-in. bomb thrower, as did most British tanks of this period. The weapon was mounted to the left of the gun, firing through a hole in the turret roof and was used to launch smoke grenades. It was controlled, in respect of range, by a valve that provided three options: 20yds, 70yds and 100yds. British stowage diagrams and a few photographs show Fireflies with a pair of the old 4-in. smoke dischargers attached externally to the right side of the turret, although these must have been rare.

January 1945: one regiment nominated to take up defensive positions in the Ardennes was 1st Northamptonshire Yeomanry. At least three Fireflies are identifiable in this chilly scene. Despite icy and snowbound roads, the regiment played an active part in Operation *Mullet*, intended to drive the remaining Germans out of the area.

SHERMAN VC FIREFLY

The drawing shows how the gun dominated the tank, leaving very little room for the crew; the driver sat alone at the front, whilst the commander, gunner and loader were crammed into the turret. When it fired the whole tank rocked back on its suspension as the gun recoiled violently within the turret.

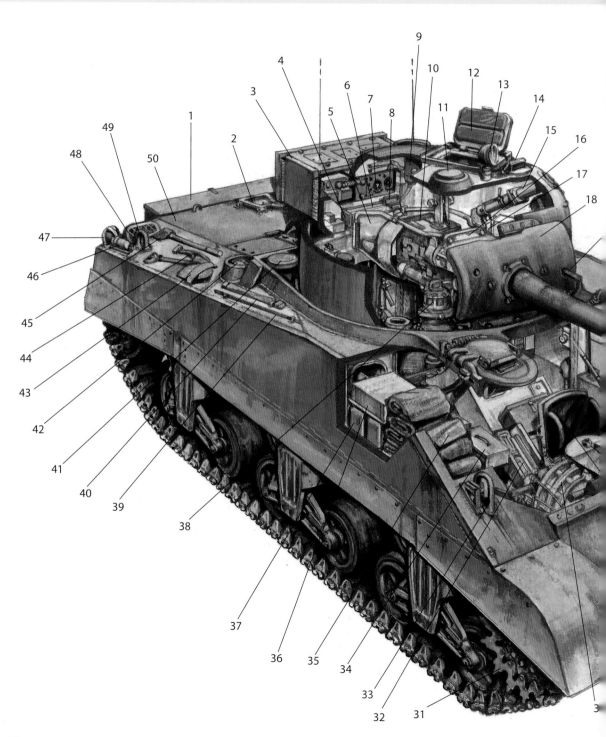

SPECIFICATIONS

Crew	4
Combat weight	34.75 tons
Overall length	25ft 6in.
Width	8ft 8in.
Height	9ft
Engine	Chrysler A57 multi-bank
Transmission	Five-speed synchromesh and controlled differential steering
Fuel capacity	160 gallons
Armament	17 Pounder Mark IV QF gun and .30-cal. Browning machine-gun
Ammunition stowage	77 rounds
Muzzle velocity	2,900 feet per second
Effective range	2,500 yards
Gen elevation/depression	20 degrees/5 degrees
Speed	22.25mph
Maximum armour thickness	3 inches

KEY

1   Rear stowage box
2   Gun support crutch
3   Armoured radio box
4   First aid box
5   Gun recoil guard
6   Sub machine-gun ammunition
7   No.19 Wireless set
8   Hellensen lamp
9   Variometer, 'A' set aerial
10 17-pounder breech ring
11 Turret ventilator
12 Loader's hatch
13 Turret spot lamp
14 Loader's periscope
15 Two-inch bomb thrower
16 Gun mounting cradle
17 Hand grenade stowage
18 Gun mantlet
19 Co-axial Browning .30-cal. machine gun
20 Hull ventilator
21 Vehicle tool stowage
22 Spare periscope heads
23 Fire extinguisher
24 Instrument panel
25 17 Pounder Mark IV QF Gun
26 Muzzle brake
27 Siren
28 Hood for driver's hatch
29 Driver's seat
30 Transmission housing
31 Track drive sprocket
32 .30-cal. machine-gun ammunition
33 Lifting ring
34 .50-cal. machine-gun ammunition
35 Blankets
36 Colman cooker
37 Two 5-gallon water cans
38 Turret traverse controls
39 Crowbar
40 Pickaxe handle
41 Ventilator
42 Fuel filler
43 Shovel
44 Pickaxe head
45 Axe
46 Methyl bromide extinguisher
47 Tail light
48 Ventilator
49 Lifting ring
50 Engine deck

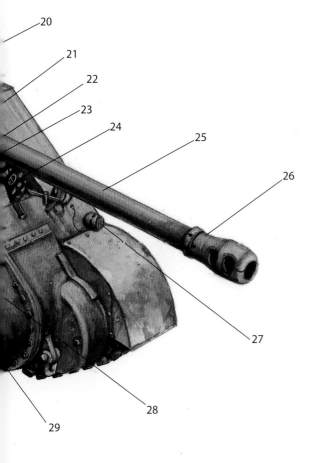

THE CONVERSION PROGRAMME

Following inspection of a prototype 17-pounder Sherman, which was available from 6 January 1944, the War Office in London issued a requirement for a total of 2,100 of the up-gunned tanks. Four Royal Ordnance factories are known to have been involved in the work: Woolwich and Hayes in the London area, Radcliffe near Manchester, and Nottingham. The numbers reflected the preponderance of Shermans in British regiments at this time, and of course, Canadian and Polish regiments that were equipped from British stocks. However, the matter became more critical once it was appreciated that the rival A30 Challenger would not be ready in time for D-Day. It had already been agreed that in the interests of commonality, Challengers would only be issued to those regiments that were destined to field the British Cromwell tank. To that end, the total order for Challengers was limited to just 200. Yet despite a head start of at least 12 months, Challenger production was in arrears, and early trials had already revealed the need for modifications. Until such time as the Challenger could be declared fit for service, those regiments slated to receive it would also have to be given Fireflies.

Compared with the Sherman Firefly, the A30 Challenger has always received a bad press. There is no doubt that it inherited most of the frailties of the Cromwell from which it was derived, exacerbated by the nature of the

Richard Harley's detailed scale drawing reveals what few would otherwise believe: that in fact, despite appearances, the A30 Challenger was marginally lower than a Firefly, or indeed any Sherman.

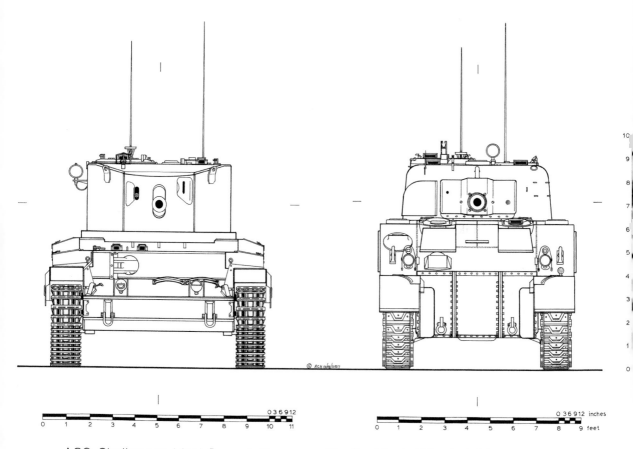

A30 Challenger Mark I and Sherman Firefly Mark VC: height comparison.

Drawn to 1:24th scale (½" = 1 foot) by Richard C. Harley. Copyright 14th August 2007.

January 1945: Operation *Blackcock* and a snow-camouflaged IC Hybrid of 1st RTR has its gun cleaned in Schilberg. From this angle, the long gun looks very foreshortened. The crewmen are wearing the thick, warm tank suit. A couple of empty shell cases have been thrown down alongside the jerrycans on the right.

conversion that seriously upset the original balance of the design. However, the most common complaint, that it was taller and therefore a more conspicuous target than the Firefly, can be shown quite simply to be false. The impression is created by the tall, flat-sided turret on a long, low hull, but that is an optical illusion.

Many sources published since the war imply that any type of Sherman could be converted to mount the 17-pounder, but this is entirely erroneous. In fact, there was a variety of factors, both technical and logistical, that limited the suitability of tanks for conversion. A document dated November 1944 lists features that were essential in a Sherman required for conversion. In the first place, apparently, only petrol-engined Shermans would do, which effectively ruled out the M4A2 (Sherman III). No reason is given, so unless there was some unexplained physical factor, then it can only have been connected with availability. There were similar restrictions in respect of petrol-engined Shermans. Evidence for the existence of a Sherman IIC – that is, a Firefly based upon the cast hull M4A1 – is scarce and difficult to substantiate from official sources, unless the type failed to qualify in some other category. It is unlikely to be due to the hull form alone since the Canadians certainly considered a Firefly conversion to their very similar Grizzly. On the other hand, the M4A3, which in Firefly mode would have been designated IVC, can safely be ruled out since it was almost exclusively a US Army tank of which the British had only a few samples. Thus, in essence, only M4 (Sherman I) and M4A4 (Sherman V) would actually qualify, assuming certain other features were acceptable.

One important feature was that any tank suitable for conversion must have the wide type of gun mantlet that was classified M34A1 in American service. The reason for this becomes clear as soon as one examines the older alternative, the narrow M34 type, which clearly could not be adapted to mount the larger gun. And finally in this list of features, the hydraulic type of turret power traverse was also considered essential.

This raises a number of interesting points. Britain had rejected hydraulic traverse gear quite early in the war in favour of electric on the grounds that if a hydraulic pipe was severed in action it constituted a fire risk. In order not to hold up Sherman production, the Americans had adopted traverse motors

16 January 1945: men of 52nd (Lowland) Division and their Carriers in Tuddern supported by a snow-camouflaged VC of Sherwood Rangers Yeomanry, 8th Armoured Brigade. The Brigade history tells us that on the eve of Operation *Blackcock*, white bedsheets and whitewash arrived to disguise their dark tanks against the snowy landscape.

by three manufacturers. One, which was electric, came from the Westinghouse Corporation. The other two, by Logansport and Oilgear, were both hydraulic systems, although the latter was far and away the better. Experienced British officers found the Westinghouse electric traverse difficult to control with sufficient finesse for fast and accurate tank gunnery, while the Logansport hydraulic system was probably too sensitive and could not deal with inconsistencies in the machining of the turret ring, for example. The Oilgear equipment, on the other hand, proved to be smooth, easy to control, and capable of overriding small inconsistencies. Thus, when hydraulic traverse gear is specified for tanks suitable for the Firefly conversion, it is safe to assume that in fact only the Oilgear system would do.

These concerns seem to be simple enough but for the fact that deliveries of Shermans from the United States were inconsistent even in the best of times. Worse still, as one report pointed out, was that even when suitable tanks had been identified from a particular batch, some might still be required to complete deliveries as 75mm gun tanks and could not be made available for conversion to Fireflies.

D **MINE-DAMAGED SHERMAN VC FIREFLY ON SCAMMELL TRMU/30 TRANSPORTER, NORMANDY, JULY 1944**

Despite popular mythology, largely generated by the cinema, tanks were not always totally destroyed if they became casualties. This Sherman Firefly has been mined. The leading suspension unit has been blasted off and the drive sprocket damaged beyond repair, but the tank itself is not a write-off. The tracks have been recovered and stowed on the tank's engine deck and even evidence of fire at the rear is probably no more than superficial.

The Scammell TRMU/30 was a classic British design with pre-war origins, designed primarily for tank recovery rather than long-distance transportation. Although officially limited to a payload of 30 tons, it proved quite capable of winching aboard and transporting a 35-ton VC Firefly to an Advanced Base Workshop of the Royal Electrical and Mechanical Engineers.

Here the tank would be inspected and, if within the scope of the ABW, returned to serviceable condition. That done, the tank would be sent on to a Forward Delivery Squadron, Royal Armoured Corps and in due course would find its way back to regimental service with a new crew and, if they could be bothered, a new set of markings.

25 March 1945 was a Sunday, but it was business as usual on the Rhine, with a Firefly from C Squadron, 4th/7th Dragoon Guards sharing a class 50/60 raft with a D8 bulldozer for the crossing to Rees. An earlier attempt to load two tanks onto one raft ended with it sinking.

To return briefly to the topic of turret traverse, it should be noted that according to some experts, the 17-pounder turret, with the counterweight at the back formed by the radio box, was actually better balanced than the standard 75mm version. A trial conducted at Lulworth with a Firefly standing on a 15-degree slope, showed that it was still possible to turn the turret by hand, albeit with a bit more effort and that the power traverse still functioned. On the other hand, traverse speeds on a 17-pounder turret appear to have been slower than the 75mm version, although this was not entirely a bad thing. Creep speed, the ultra-slow traverse required for the fine laying of a gun onto its target, was measured at .125 degrees per second against .20 degrees per second of a regular Sherman with the same equipment. Not a significant difference but clearly a critical advantage for a Firefly gunner.

This raises another significant point because in addition to balancing the turret itself, it was also necessary to balance the gun in the turret. In fact, balance, in this case, was a relative term: ideally the gun should be slightly breech heavy. With the regular canvas holder hanging from the recoil guard behind the breech ring to catch ejected shell cases, the 17-pounder mounting was 450lb muzzle heavy. To correct this, it would have been necessary to add 92lb of weight to balance the longer gun. Instead, a perforated metal container was fitted in lieu of canvas and provided most of the necessary weight, although there was provision to add small balance weights to the rear of the recoil guard. Of course, despite the fact that the gun was well balanced in the turret, it proved impossible to fire on the move, so the stabilizing gear fitted to a regular Sherman was removed.

AMMUNITION

For most of their service, Sherman Fireflies were supplied with three types of ammunition: APC (Armour Piercing Capped), APCBC (Armour Piercing Capped Ballistic Capped), and HE (High Explosive). Since they are the subject of much pointless argument, precise performance figures will be avoided as much as possible, but it is safe to say that the APCBC round was a modest improvement in terms of accuracy and penetration on the APC

4 April 1945: a Firefly of the Scots Greys, with extended end connectors on the tracks, crosses the Dortmund–Ems Canal on a Bailey Bridge. Allied armour was now deep inside Germany, and the end more or less in sight, but still the official censor thought it necessary to hide the identity of the regiment by obliterating the insignia.

round but that this difference decreased as the range increased. Regular AP (Armour Piercing) shot, which was available for the anti-tank gun, was not, apparently, carried in the tanks. APC was virtually the same round with a hardened cap on the nose to improve penetration, while APCBC had an additional pointed cap to improve aerodynamic performance.

High explosive was the problem. Backed by a conventional charge, the 17-pounder could fire a high explosive round out to a range of 10,000yds, way beyond the normal fighting range of tanks. This was fine if the tanks were to be used in the long-range artillery role that both Briggs and Witheridge had favoured, but that was in the desert. The long view was not available in Europe, where fighting ranges reduced dramatically, yet there was still a need for high explosive. Indeed, figures published at the end of the war showed that Allied tanks used far more high explosive ammunition than

12 April 1945: C Squadron, Coldstream Guards wait on the road to Bremen while a spot of bother is cleared up in the woods on the right. The nearest tank is a Firefly equipped with Typhoon rockets that were unique to this squadron. On the right side of the turret the launch rail is empty but the tail of a rocket can be seen on the left.

armour piercing in the course of the campaign. The solution seemed to be to reduce the charge in the high explosive cartridge so that the projectile would not fly so far. However, the result of this was that a shell impacting on soft ground did not have enough force behind it to set off the nose fuse, and so the shell failed to detonate. The problem was resolved in due course, although the Firefly was primarily a tank fighting tank and stood or fell by the armour-piercing performance of its gun.

In August 1944, a new round appeared: APDS (Armour Piercing Discarding Sabot), a solid tungsten core surrounded by a light casing that filled the calibre of the gun. As it left the muzzle, this casing, with the full charge of the cartridge behind it, broke away from the core (at some risk to anyone in the immediate vicinity), enabling the core to proceed on its way with less air resistance due to its smaller size. The results could be impressive. In theory, even the thick, sloped frontal armour of the massive Tiger II could be penetrated at ranges up to 1,500yds – if one could hit it. The trouble was that, certainly in the early days, APDS became chronically inaccurate at anything above about 500yds, which was a suicidal range for any Sherman to fight from. Accuracy improved in due course, but that was not the only problem.

For one thing, due to its shape, the APDS round was liable to foul the baffles in the 17-pounder's muzzle brake. These had to be altered. It also tended to clog up the rifling with tiny shards of metal, and this could ruin the accuracy of subsequent APCBC rounds that might be fired. This was duly reported and the Americans notified, but there was no easy answer. One theory considered having dedicated APDS tanks, but that always raised the problem of ensuring that the right tank was in the right place at the right time – and there are special laws that govern that sort of thing.

1. M4A3 WITH BRITISH FIREFLY TURRET, ARMY GROUND FORCES BOARD, FORT KNOX, KENTUCKY, 1944

At least two complete Firefly turrets were sent to North America, one apparently to Canada where it appears to have been fitted to a Grizzly, Canada's version of the M4A1 Sherman. The other went to the United States, specifically the Army Ground Forces Board at Fort Knox, Kentucky. Here it was mounted on an otherwise unadapted M4A3 hull for trials.

American experience of the Firefly in north-west Europe is covered in the main text but we do not know the results of these tests. One assumes that the box on the rear of the turret was the standard British version, designed to accommodate the No.19 set and therefore a bit too small to contain the American radio.

At some stage the turret was transferred to an M4A2 hull and in this guise it survives in the collection of the Ordnance Museum, Aberdeen Proving Ground, Maryland.

2. SHERMAN IC FIREFLY, HEADQUARTERS SQUADRON, PRETORIA REGIMENT, 6TH SOUTH AFRICAN ARMOURED DIVISION, ITALY, MAY 1945

South African 6th Armoured Division was formed in 1942 but, due largely to manpower problems, was not ready to move to Italy until April 1944. By the end of the war the regiment, indeed probably all three regiments of 11th South African Armoured Brigade, had been issued with the Firefly's American equivalent, the M4A1 with 76mm gun in the T23 turret, the Sherman IIA in British service. The Fireflies may have been concentrated in HQ Squadron in order to rationalize the distribution of ammunition. With their reduced crews they would hardly be ideal for any sort of command function but they would probably still represent the most potent firepower in the regiment.

The South African Shermans in Italy appear to have been painted a dark green towards the end of the war and as second in the brigade the Pretoria Regiment would bear the number 52 in conjunction with the divisional sign, a green and yellow triangle (the national colours) and display squadron signs in yellow.

CONCRETE BUSTERS

Back in May 1943, while George Brighty was still struggling to get a 17-pounder gun to fit inside a Sherman turret, a trial took place at Shoeburyness, the artillery testing ground on the north shore of the Thames Estuary. The trial involved six of the 17-pounder anti-tank guns, all firing armour-piercing rounds at a reinforced concrete wall about 7ft 6in. thick. Among the observers was LtCol O'Rorke, commander of the Gunnery School at Lulworth, who was clearly there to represent Royal Armoured Corps interest.

Apparently, there was not much to see while the guns were firing, just a huge cloud of dust. But when the test was over, the result seems to have disappointed many of the observers. Rounds had certainly penetrated the concrete, indeed there was a great gap in the wall like an inverted triangle, but the steel reinforcing bars were still in place, and there was a ramp of rubble at the base. Since the object of breaking down the wall was to enable a tank to get through, it is odd that no tank was present to try its luck, but the watchers had their doubts. It may have been difficult for a tank to climb over the rubble because the gap at the base of the wall was much too narrow, and no one could be sure whether the reinforcing bars would stop the tank or not. A request was made for a Churchill tank to be available next time, but it is not clear whether there was a next time or not.

It is surprising, therefore, to discover that the very first action involving Sherman Fireflies was in a concrete busting role on the early morning of D-Day itself. How it came about is unclear, and all we know for sure is that on the morning of 6 June 1944, among the Tank Landing Craft heading for the Normandy beaches were three of the short but beamy Landing Craft Tank Mark 5 (LCT[5]). They are believed to have been fitted with a raised section of deck at the forward end of the tank deck so that the Fireflies could fire over the lip of the bow ramp. A similar arrangement was made for the Centaur tanks of the Royal Marine Armoured Support Group (see New Vanguard 104).

28 April 1945: C Squadron, Coldstream Guards sporting their famous Tulip rockets halted near Westerimke prisoner of war camp. In the foreground a Sherman IC Firefly displays a camouflaged gun barrel, a disguise of dubious value in most situations.

A private snapshot of an M4A4 VC Firefly of 5th Royal Tank Regiment at rest in an orchard with suitable foliage attached to the turret. The domestic arrangements suggest that the crew are experienced at making themselves comfortable. This crew likes its beverages: there is a coffee pot on the ground and a kettle dangling from the back of the tank.

Surviving evidence suggests that one LCT carrying a pair of Fireflies was part of the assault force that approached Sword Beach, while two more were allotted to the Canadian regiments that were heading for Juno. No evidence can be found for their use on Gold Beach. On paper, the six tanks were on the establishment of 259 Tank Delivery Squadron, although in fact each pair was allocated to a Sherman DD regiment (see Osprey New Vanguard 123: *Swimming Shermans*). These were the British 13th/18th Hussars and two Canadian regiments, the 1st Hussars (6th Canadian Armoured Regiment) and Fort Garry Horse (10th Canadian Armoured Regiment). Each tank was crewed by a reserve crew from the relevant regiment.

The intention was clearly to engage specific concrete defences on the beach during the run in. Shooting accurately from tanks on the moving decks of relatively small craft might be regarded as impossible, but it appears to have worked, at least in the case of the 1st Hussars. Each tank stood on the raised deck with a good stock of spare ammunition alongside and extra men to pass it up to the loader as required, presumably in order that when the tanks landed they would still be fully stowed. One assumes that the tanks would be

The visual evidence suggests that this Hybrid IC Firefly belonged to B Squadron, Vth Inniskilling Dragoon Guards. The square on the turret tells us the squadron; the red jerboa of 7th Armoured Division shows up on the front stowage box, nearside. On the other side, one can just make out the stag's head of 22nd Armoured Brigade facing upwards, and beneath it what could be '52' or '53'. The name St Michael sounds appropriate for the Skins.

Another fascinating snapshot showing two Fireflies, both with camouflaged guns but different hull forms. Inevitably, these private photographs were taken when the tanks and their crews were at rest, revealing the domestic arrangements. Brackets like the one across the front of the nearest tank seem to have been favoured by 5th RTR.

equipped with deep wading gear because once the landing craft touched down, the Firefly crews were instructed to go ashore, finish off the obstacles they had been shooting at, and then join up with their parent regiments. Thus, for example, the two Fireflies of 13th/18th Hussars (which according to reports did not fire at all on the way in) joined up respectively with A and B, the DD Squadrons, to stiffen up their firepower in the event that any heavy German tanks were encountered.

To round off the story of the DD regiments on D-Day: they were followed ashore some 45 minutes later by the tanks of their regimental headquarters and their third, non-swimming, squadron. This last would be equipped with Fireflies on the scale of one per troop, but once they were all ashore and out of action, Fireflies would be delivered for the DD squadrons on the same scale. From now on, they would be organized and would fight like regular Sherman regiments.

F **LANDING CRAFT TANK (5) CB No.2337, 330TH SUPPORT FLOTILLA CARRYING TWO SHERMAN VC FIREFLIES OF 259 DELIVERY SQUADRON, OFF SWORD BEACH, NORMANDY, 6 JUNE 1944**

As explained in the text this curious business has only recently enjoyed any serious publicity and a lot of questions remain to be answered. Contemporary records from the D-Day period indicate just three of these craft: two with the Canadians on Juno and one with the 13th/18th Hussars on Sword, the two tanks manned by crews from that regiment. None are associated with Gold sector but the Americans seem to have had a similar arrangement, with 75mm gun Shermans, on Omaha.

The American-built LCT(5) was a good deal smaller than other classes of LCT and its capacity was limited to four or five tanks at most, depending on weight. In this role the raised deck section must have added to the weight and, as far as one can tell, this example, destined for Sword, only carried the two Fireflies. However they would be something like one metre higher than normal, which must have upset the vessel's stability.

The tanks would have been waterproofed in order to wade ashore, yet one assumes that this did not include the turret ring or mantlet area since the gun would need to traverse and elevate during the run in. It is understood that in this case the tanks did not engage any targets on the way in, although this has not been explained. They were under orders to join up with the two DD squadrons of their regiment once ashore but they are not mentioned in the regimental history and nothing more is known of them from this point.

13 June 1944: this Firefly, apparently in an ambush position, belongs to the Staffordshire Yeomanry. The regiment, part of 27th Armoured Brigade, landed on D-Day and played a key part in preventing 21st Panzer Division from reaching the beachhead. Its Fireflies were VC (M4A4), while the rest of its Shermans were the diesel M4A2 variant.

There was, of course, one non-DD regiment equipped with Shermans that landed on D-Day. This was the Staffordshire Yeomanry, otherwise the Queen's Own Royal Regiment, which formed part of 27th Armoured Brigade. One looks to them as, hopefully, a fruitful source of early use of the Firefly. But one looks in vain. The regimental war diary tells us that in June 1944, they were equipped with 48 M4A2 (Sherman III) and 12 M4A4 (Sherman V), which must have been their Fireflies because the diesel-powered M4A2 was considered unsuitable for conversion. Since the Staffordshire Yeomanry played a significant part in frustrating the advance of the 21st Panzer Division against the beachhead, it is a pity that more particular information on the use of their Fireflies is not available. At least we can rely on one good photograph to prove that the regiment did have Fireflies.

THE FIREFLY IN ACTION

Even if we cannot confirm that the Staffordshire Yeomanry was probably the first regiment to employ Fireflies in combat, it seems a reasonable bet. On the other hand, it appears that impressions gleaned at the time were not always reliable. For example, the Sherwood Rangers came to the conclusion within a few days of landing that the Germans were singling out their Fireflies for priority destruction, presumably on account of their longer guns. This is not an unreasonable assumption, but it is not borne out by the evidence. According to a British report dated 23 June 1944, the total 'wastage', as they put it, of Fireflies in one Canadian and three British armoured brigades ashore, was 19 per cent of the total available compared with 29 per cent of their regular tanks – and that includes 22nd Armoured Brigade in 7th Armoured Division, which had lost 101 Cromwells against just six Fireflies by that date. Surely, if there was anywhere that the Fireflies would stick out, it was while mixing with flocks of the comparatively diminutive Cromwells. On the other hand, as far as regular tanks were concerned, much of this wastage had already been made good: of 264 tanks knocked out 188 had already been replaced. Where Fireflies were concerned, 22 had been lost, but as of 23 June, only six had arrived as replacements.

A pristine IC M4 Firefly undergoing trials at the Mechanization Experimental Establishment at Ottariano in Italy. Every hatch is open, including that of the absent hull machine gunner and it is clear that this tank, perhaps the first Firefly to arrive in Italy, is fitted with rubber block tracks.

Such statistics are always cold-blooded. They mask a great deal of pain. It is more heartening to read of some complimentary user opinion. Colonel Readman, commanding the Royal Scots Greys in 4th Armoured Brigade – which was not included in the statistics above – reported his initial reaction to the Firefly on 24 July 1944. He says that based on experience in Italy, where heavy German tanks such as the Pz Kpfw V Panther and Pz Kpfw VI Tiger were rare, the regiment had been minded to organize its Fireflies into separate troops, each troop to provide long-range cover to three troops of 75mm Shermans in each squadron. Experience in Normandy, where one seemed to find a Panther or Tiger waiting around every corner, resulted in a rapid reorganization, so that each tank troop had a Firefly of its own. While they were in short supply, this seems to have been common practice, but Col Readman looked forward to a time when each troop in his regiment would have three Fireflies to one 75mm Sherman, which would be there to provide high explosive or smoke. Indeed, Readman said, if sufficient Fireflies were not available, he would be prepared to take M10 self-propelled guns armed with the 17-pounder instead.

Individual crew experiences are rarely reliable, no matter how interesting they might be, for the simple reason that one individual in a tank has little idea of what is going on around him, never mind farther away. As a result, where we are obliged to be concise, a more general source is better. One of the best was compiled by Col W. E. H. Grylls in 1945 for Brigadier Charles Dunphie, Deputy Commander of the Royal Armoured Corps. Grylls clearly had a lot of experience of tank combat in north-west Europe and had sounded many crews for their views. This experience enabled him to place things in perspective and give a reasonably dispassionate appraisal.

For example, he estimated that despite the many unkind things said about it, the Chrysler multi-bank engine was a lot more reliable than it was ever given credit for, particularly by those who had to service it. He reveals that on early Fireflies the muzzle brake had a tendency to work loose because the locking device was not satisfactory. He also says that in Normandy, Fireflies suffered a number of traverse gear failures because the gear was not capable of handling the greater weight. However, he claims that the Department of Tank Design had already appreciated this and soon had an improved type

Crossing a Bailey Bridge in Italy, this Firefly belongs to 18th New Zealand Armoured Regiment. The turret is reversed, the gun barrel supported in its crutch, and with plenty of stowage attached. Notice too that there is a substantial towing attachment at the rear.

ready. Another interesting conclusion concerns the risk of fire in Fireflies. Despite an enduring belief that this was due in the main to petrol fuel, trials had clearly shown that in fact the most important factor was the way that ammunition was stowed. Until the Americans introduced wet stowage, the Shermans were particularly vulnerable in this respect since ammunition was stowed all around the fighting compartment, easy to reach in a hurry but just as easily hit if the tank's armour was penetrated. In the Firefly, where much of the ammunition was located below the turret floor, it was a lot less exposed, so that fires in Fireflies were uncommon, relatively speaking.

1. SHERMAN VC FIREFLY, 19TH ARMOURED REGIMENT, 4TH NEW ZEALAND ARMOURED BRIGADE, ITALY APRIL 1945

Having experienced the muddy conditions of an Italian winter, 2nd New Zealand Armoured Brigade applied locally made Platypus grousers made from lengths of angle iron fixed to the tracks and extended outwards for quite a long way; even after the weather improved, the New Zealanders seem to have retained them on their tanks. They were certainly seen on 17-pounder Shermans operated by the Brigade as late as April 1945. This impressive front view shows a Sherman VC, so equipped, thundering along an Italian highway.

The 17-pounder gun has been camouflage painted to try to disguise its length and this tank has patches of appliqué armour fitted ahead of the driver's and redundant co-driver's positions. There is also a .30-cal. M1919 Browning machine gun mounted on the commander's cupola. New Zealand Shermans are reported to have been painted in a shade similar to US olive drab although this would soon acquire a patina of local dust.

2. SHERMAN IC HYBRID FIREFLY ZEMSTA II (REVENGE) OF C SQUADRON, 1ST KRECHOWIECKI LANCERS, 2ND POLISH ARMOURED BRIGADE, ITALY 1944

From this angle the bulbous front end of a Hybrid Sherman IC (M4) shows up clearly as it eases its way across a Churchill ARK. Like most tanks in the Polish 2nd Armoured Division, this one has a name painted boldly in yellow on the side of the hull and yet employs the approved method of camouflage on the gun barrel. The hull also features patches of appliqué armour covering the regular areas but not on the turret.

The ARK is simply a redundant Churchill tank hull with hinged ramps at each end that would be driven into a gap to provide a causeway for other tanks to cross. They appear to have been popular in Italy, yet there is no evidence for their use in north-west Europe. Those used in Italy had exposed tracks that service tanks would normally drive over but in this case planks have been laid to provide a smooth surface.

A small fascine in the form of a tightly bound bundle of sticks is seen on the nose of the tank to be used for crossing a muddy ditch or similar obstacle, but otherwise the front end of this tank is remarkably free of clutter.

1

2

This unusual photograph shows tanks of C Squadron, 2nd RTR, in Italy. It is remarkable because the squadron is operating a mixture of Fireflies, notably the second tank in line, and Shermans equipped with the American 76mm gun in the enlarged turret, such as *Cameron*, in the foreground. Naturally, there will be 75mm gun tanks in the line as well so that the quartermaster is faced with handling at least three different types of ammunition.

There are other things that Grylls does not mention. For example, many crews reported that the flash at the muzzle when the gun fired obscured the view of the target and made it difficult to ensure that they had hit it. Grylls says that it was normal practice to fire at an enemy tank until it caught fire, thus making sure that it was destroyed, so perhaps that was not quite such a problem. From the crews' point of view, it was a flash at the breech end that bothered them, despite being informed loftily by the Medical Research Council that it would not do them any harm. Even so, a canvas curtain was installed to shield the loader, and it was suggested that the turret crew might be issued with hoods to protect them, such as those worn by naval turret personnel. However, common sense and ingenuity prevailed when George Witheridge modified the electrics to create a delayed action breech that was introduced as the Mark VII gun. Another small but irritating fault reported by some crews was that rain leaked into the radio box on the back of the turret, presumably around the lid on top. None of this did anything to diminish the popularity of the Firefly, and the demand for more continued. Indeed, from statements he made at the time, it appears that Field Marshal Montgomery believed that ultimately Fireflies would replace 75mm gun tanks in all British regiments. In practice, the best that any regiment achieved, and probably as many as they required, was two per troop because the greater versatility of the 75mm gun continued to be appreciated.

Italy was another theatre where the firepower of the Firefly would be welcome, but its demands could not be met until those of 21st Army Group had been satisfied. The demands became more urgent and the calls for them more strident as time went on. As the Allied armies moved north, encounters with heavier German tanks became more common, but it was October 1944 before Fireflies could be spared for that theatre. By the time these had been shared out between British, Canadian, New Zealand, Polish and South African regiments, one per troop was the best that could be hoped for and the most they ever managed.

Perhaps for this reason, regiments in the Italian theatre treasured their Fireflies all the more. They certainly went to far greater lengths to camouflage them than did their counterparts in northern Europe who relied on disruptive painting and a trick of the light to confuse the enemy. It was the gun, of course, that was the problem. Some senior officers had already criticized it for the way it stuck out in front of the tank, entirely missing the point that it was the length of the barrel, more than anything else, that ensured the high velocity and hitting power of the weapon.

Trying to disguise the gun was not easy. Camouflage experts in Italy accepted the concept of paint and even embellished it by fitting a device midway along the barrel that looked like a muzzle brake. Whether it would have fooled anyone, any of the time, is open to question, but at least it was not as drastic as the alternative. This was for the tank to operate as much as possible with the turret traversed aft and the barrel camouflaged with suitable vegetation on the engine deck. Meanwhile, a dummy 75mm gun, fitted to the rear of the turret was supposed to fool the Germans into thinking that this was an ordinary Sherman they were dealing with. The trouble was that one could only maintain this deception for so long: at some point the big gun had

A very odd arrangement indeed: an M4A4 Sherman V that is pretending to be a Firefly, with a long dummy gun paralleling the real one and a box on the rear of the turret. Unfortunately, we cannot see whether a loader's hatch has been added or the hull machine gun blanked off. Why on Earth should anyone do this?

to be traversed forwards in order to do its business, and then the cat was out of the bag. Logic seems to suggest that if the tank was close enough to the enemy for the dummy gun to be seen, then it was time to have the real gun facing forwards, loaded and ready for action.

Perhaps because they were farther from the seat of power, troops in Italy displayed a degree of independence that was not so evident in north-west Europe. One example will suffice. The 2nd Lothian and Border Horse, in 26th Armoured Brigade, did not take kindly to the idea of dumping a crew member, and so they went into action with the fifth man stuffed into the front with the extra ammunition. Obviously, he had nothing to do because the machine gun had been removed. The practice was portrayed as an example of team spirit, which it undoubtedly was, but there may have been a secondary agenda: work shared between five men was easier than between four.

The presence of a Comet in the background suggests 29th Armoured Brigade towards the end of the war in Germany. However, the cap badges, along with the visible markings of this crew and their Firefly, seem to indicate 5th RTR in 22nd Armoured Brigade.

THE AMERICAN ANGLE

Raymond Briggs, in a report compiled on his return from the United States, reckoned that the Firefly had to some extent re-established British credibility in American eyes. There had been a lot of criticism before this time because the Americans believed that the British were wasting good tanks by adapting them to other roles and then demanding more. Now at last the Americans saw an adaptation that they could approve of. Not that they had any more direct interest in the tank: they had something similar of their own.

The American 76mm, in contrast to its British counterpart, had been developed as a tank gun and only later adapted to a towed mounting. Like the British weapon, it was in fact 76.2mm calibre, or 3in. It was part of a programme launched in summer 1943 to develop the 'ultimate' Sherman, although the Americans could afford a more wholehearted approach than the British and created what was, in effect, a new tank with a new and bigger turret to take the longer gun.

The adoption of the new gun seems to be a tacit admission on the Americans' part that defeating enemy armour was an important function of a tank after all, but that did not impress everyone. Indeed, in the lead up to D-Day there was a marked reluctance on the part of some US Army units to part with their 75mm gun tanks because they valued the dual role of the older gun. Experience of the heavier German tanks, notably the Panther, soon changed that. One can imagine the disappointment when it was discovered that the armour-piercing performance did not come up to expectations. The reverberations reached the top. General Eisenhower is recorded as saying, 'Ordnance told me this 76 would take care of anything the Germans had. Now I find you can't knock out a damn thing with it.' An exaggeration of course, but it is indicative of the frustration felt among American tank men that individually, their tanks were no match for the Germans' best.

As a result, the Americans developed what they called a High Velocity Armour Piercing (HVAP) round – what the British would call APCR, or Armour Piercing Composite Rigid – that relied on a core of tungsten to do the damage. Even this had a poor record when tested on a captured Panther,

This VC Firefly was one of three or four that fell into German hands at various times. What appears to be a number 6 is in fact 'G' for *Guss*, meaning cast armour, while 'W' is *Walzstahl*, which indicates areas of rolled (or flat) plate; presumably for instructional purposes. Apart from an A Squadron triangle on the turret and a bold War Department number on the side of the hull, there are no other indications of the previous owners.

and it was always in short supply. General Omar Bradley decided that what the Americans needed was the Sherman Firefly.

A letter from US 12th Army dated 13 August 1944 requests that sufficient Fireflies be made available until such time as the new American 90mm gun was ready or improved ammunition for the 76mm gun was issued. In all respects, it was a forlorn hope. The British were struggling to produce enough Fireflies for themselves, the Canadians and the Poles in France, and the Italian theatre was also demanding them. The Americans were a long way down the list. In the United States, British liaison officer Brig G. McLeod Ross suggested that the 17-pounder gun should be mounted in the larger T23 turret, designed for the 76mm Sherman, but mounted on the new American T26 chassis. This was turned down on the grounds that the T23 turret was inadequate in terms of armour, and the alternative – to fit the 17-pounder into the T26 turret in place of the designed weapon, the 90mm – was regarded as a waste of effort; all this despite the fact that it was believed that the British gun would outperform the larger American gun. One report said, 'It will doubtless take a lot of pressure to make the USA adopt the 17-pr, but it would be well worth while.'

Evidence for the existence of the American Firefly is by no means comprehensive, but there is sufficient documentation in print to provide a reasonable picture. Naturally, due to the supply situation, it was 1945 before anything concrete was done. However, an initial requirement is specified for 100 Fireflies based on M4, M4A1 and M4A3, all of course, with the M34A1 gun mount and Oilgear power traverse. At some point, undated, two M4A3 tanks were taken from US Army stocks at Tidworth on Salisbury Plain for conversion to mount the British 17-pounder. One of these is recorded as having armoured ammunition stowage and one with 'wet', that is to say, Glycol stowage. Whether these can be regarded as prototypes for the American Firefly is not clear, but there are a number of interesting specifications. For example, a larger armoured box is required on the back of the turret because the American SCR 508 radio is bigger than the British No.19 set, and the Americans also require stowage clips for a Browning M2 heavy machine gun on the back of this box. Furthermore, they specify their M9 elevating quadrant to replace the British Clinometer.

It was one thing to issue a requirement for tanks but quite another to find them. On 9 March 1945, 22 Shermans arrived at Southampton, presumably from stocks in France. A convoy of 26 tank transporters awaited them at the docks, and they were soon on their way to Woolwich for conversion. Whether this was the first batch is not clear, but further records, often detailed down to individual tank numbers, are for similar quantities. On 11 March, the full requirement was specified as 160 Fireflies. About a month later, on 8 April, this was halved to 80, and it was suggested that the balance could be converted to flails (see New Vanguard 139: *Sherman Crab Flail Tank*). The last word is a document issued on 26 May 1945, and it states that 86 tanks, M4 and M4A3, equipped with the 17-pounder gun, were in theatre. It recommended that due to a shortage of ammunition, they should be issued to occupation troops in Germany or 'offered elsewhere', whatever that might have meant.

SUPPLY AND DEMAND

The American plan to upgrade the Sherman also affected Firefly production for the British Army. Since it was not considered suitable for combat by the Americans, the M4A4 (Sherman V) was not included in their 76mm gun programme, and production of the 75mm version was due to cease. This alarmed the British, who had grown to like it and even regarded it as one of their most reliable tanks – which under the circumstances might not be saying very much. As a consequence, a good deal of pressure was put on the Americans to keep the tank in production. All the same, 75mm Shermans of any type were in short supply, and Firefly conversions dropped off

May 1945: it is quite surprising to discover that immediately after the war ended in Europe, the British Army arranged a major display in Paris. This M4 (IC) Firefly, presumably from a Canadian regiment, stands polished to a high standard with the muzzle brake burnished and gleaming. Field Marshal Montgomery strolls by with a bevy of Allied officers.

9 June 1945: Montgomery again, in a smartly turned out half-track, passes a long row of Fireflies when he inspects Guards Armoured Division at Rottenburg as they prepare to disband. Many criticized the idea of putting Guardsmen in tanks, arguing that they were too rigid in their training. The Division proved them wrong.

dramatically in the third quarter of 1944. They only got going again when a new supply of suitable tanks was tapped. This was a curious version of the basic M4 (Sherman I) built by the Detroit Arsenal, featuring a combination cast and welded hull that looked a bit like an M4A1 from the front and a regular M4 from the back. The British called it the Sherman I Hybrid.

This problem had started to raise its head as early as August 1944. The workforce at Woolwich had already experienced two breaks in the production of Fireflies due to a shortage of suitable tanks. The result had a negative psychological effect: when people went to work and found nothing to do, they tended to drift away and take jobs elsewhere. In the face of a third break, the authorities decided to close down the Firefly production line at Hayes and divert the work to Woolwich. The theory was that with a reliable flow of tanks for conversion, the pace and quality of work would be maximized. Clearly, the matter was resolved because in returns from 21st Army Group early in 1945, Sherman IC tanks, most likely Hybrids, outnumbered the VC.

WHAT'S IN A NAME?

The origin of the name Firefly and its use to describe the 17-pounder armed Sherman seems to engender a lot more interest than is perhaps justified. The name was previously coined for the ridiculous installation of a 6-pounder gun in a Morris Light Reconnaissance Car, and it seems impossible to deduce any connection with the tank. Even so, the name appears to have been in fairly common usage from about March 1944 to describe the 17-pounder Sherman irrespective of mark. It will not be found on any official publications, although it appears in some war diaries, which suggests that the name was used among the troops.

The true firefly is an insect with a type of phosphorous appendage, and so there is no obvious connection there – except maybe an unconscious one. Presumably, like most insects, the firefly enjoys a short but brilliant life, and the same may be said of the tank. The Sherman Firefly fired its first shot in anger on 6 June 1944, and its last, as a frontline tank, probably in May 1945, being in the spotlight for about 11 months. True, some were passed on to other armies, and they may well have seen some action, but that is not the same thing.

The British Army shed its stock of Shermans very quickly after the war, although the 17-pounder gun remained in service with the first Centurions for a while. Yet there is no denying that the Firefly made its mark in the brief time of its service. It is easily recognizable (from the right angle), and it was the instrument of some remarkable and heroic deeds. However, if one is looking for a meaningful explanation of the tank's importance, it is probably because, at last, British troops could go out looking for Panthers and Tigers with every hope of killing them. When the Germans dominated the battlefield, with exotically named tanks of fearsome power, the Firefly, albeit a late arrival, was regarded as the antidote. It may be worth adding that in 1953 a report was issued by the Fighting Vehicle Research and Development Establishment at Chertsey with the title 'Tests of a Rigidly Mounted 17 PR. Gun'. Two of the signatures on the cover were G. H. Brighty and W. G. K. Kilbourn. Perhaps the last word can be left to MajGen Sir Campbell Clarke, the Director General of Artillery from 1942 to 1945. Writing in the *Daily Telegraph* after the war he said, 'The 17 pdr Shermans were under-armoured, but were very reliable mechanically, unlike the Tigers which they could outpace, out-manoeuvre and also outshoot.'

8 June 1946: two immaculate Fireflies devoid of any unit markings roll by the saluting base during the huge London Victory Parade. Compare the front plates of the two tanks: closest to the camera, the original model with the bolted final drive cover, while the other features the single-piece cast type. A board on the side of the nearest tank only tells us that it is a Sherman.

INDEX

References to illustrations are shown in **bold**. Plates are shown with page numbers in brackets.

A29, A30 and A34 tank specifications 8–9
America, responses to Firefly 43–45
armour protection **A1** (6), 10–11

Briggs, MajGen Raymond 12, 43
Brighty, Maj George 9, 11, 47
British Army:
    Armoured Bde, 4th, Royal Scots
      Greys 37
    Armoured Bde, 22nd 36, **42**
    Armoured Bde, 26th, 2nd Lothian
      and Border Horse 42
    Armoured Bde 27th 36, **36**
    Armoured Div, 7th 36
    Guards Armoured Div, 1st
      Coldstream Guards **A2** (6), 20, 32
    Hussars, 13th/18th 33, 34
    Royal Tank Regt, 2nd, C Sqn 40
    Royal Tank Regt, 5th 33, 42, 43
    Sherwood Rangers Yeomanry 20, 36
    Staffordshire Yeomanry 36, **36**
    Tank Delivery Sqn, 259: 33, **F** (34)

Canadian Army:
    Armoured Regt, 6th (1st Hussars) 33
    Armoured Regt, 10th (Fort Garry
      Horse) 33
    Armoured Regt, 21st (Governor
      General's Foot Guards) **A1** (6)
Centaur tank 32
Centurian tank 9
Challenger (A30) tank 9, 10–11,
    24–25, **24**
Churchill ARK **G2** (38–39)
Churchill tank 32
Clarke, MajGen Sir Campbell 47
Comet tank 9
Cromwell tank 5, 11, 36
Crusader tank 4

D-Day (6 June 1944) 32–34, **34**
Department of Tank Design (DTD) 11,
    37–38
Devers, Gen Jacob 10

equipment, radio sets 14–16, **16**, 28, 44

Firefly, Sherman
    in action 9, 17, 18, 29, 36–42, **36**, **38**
      D-Day role (6 June 1944)
        32–34, **34**
    American responses to 43–45
    ammunition 16, 18–20, **18**, 28–30, 38
      Armour Piercing Capped (APC) 28–29
      Armour Piercing Capped Ballistic
        Capped (APCBC) 28–29, 30

Armour Piercing Composite Rigid
    43–44
Armour Piercing Discarding Sabot
    (APDS) 30
conversion programmes 24–28, 44–46
crew experiences 37, 42
design 13–21
gun mantlet 25–26
name of 46–47
radio box 14–16, **16**, 28, 44
turret 25–26, 28, **E** (30–31)
    and gun mounting 16, 18–21, 28, 44
weapons
    17-pounder gun 5–9, 13, **18**, 28, **G1**
      (38), 41–42, **42**, 44
    bomb thrower 21
    Browning .30-in. machine gun **18**, 21
    smoke dischargers 21
    tulip rockets **A2** (6), 32
    Typhoon rockets 29
Firefly, IC (M4) **A2** (6), **E2** (31), 32, 37,
    41, 45
Firefly, IC Hybrid 10, 20, 25, 33, **G2**
    (38), 41, 46
Firefly, VC Firefly (M4A4) **12**, **13**,
    D (22–23), 33, **G1** (38–39), 41,
    44, **44**
    armour protection **A1** (6)
    captured (*Beute-Panzer*) 13, **B1** (14)
    Churchill ARK **G2** (38–39)
    conversions 5, 8
    damaged, on Scammell TRMU/30
      transporter **D** (26–27)
    during liberation of Netherlands
      B1 (14), **18**
    height comparison 24
Fort Knox, Kentucky 10

Grant tank 9
German Army, 21st Panzer Division 36
Grizzly tank (Canada) **E1** (30)
Grylls, Col W. E. H. 37, 40

High Explosive (HE) ammunition 28,
    29–30
High Velocity Armour Piercing (HVAP)
    ammunition 43–44

Italy 40–42

Kilbourn, Mr W. G. K. 13, 47

Landing Craft Tank (5) (LCT[5]) 32–33
    CB No.2337, 30th Support Flotilla
    F (34–35)

Montgomery, Field Marshal 40, 45, 46

New Zealand Army, 4th Armoured Bde
    G1 (38)

Operation *Blackcock* 25
Operation *Mullett* 21

Panther IV tank (German) 8
Panther V tank (German) 37
Polish Army:
    Armoured Brigade, 2nd,
      1st Krechowiecki Lancers **G2** (38)
    Armoured Division, 1st **12**

Readman, Col 37
Ross, Brig G. Mcleod 44
Royal Armoured Corps Gunnery School,
    Lulworth 9, 10–11
Royal Ordnance Factories 16–17, 24

Scammell TRMU/30 transporter
    D (26–27)
Sherman tanks
    75mm gun tanks 17, 18, 37, 40, 45
    fire risk 38
    Sherman I (M4) 25, 46
    Sherman II (M4A1) 25, **E1** (30, 31)
    Sherman IIA (M4A1) **E2** (30, 31)
    Sherman IIC 25
    Sherman III (M4A2) (76mm gun) 25,
      36, 40, 43
    Sherman IV (M4A3) 25, **E1** (30, 31), 44
    Sherman V (M4A4) 18, 25, 36, 44
    weapons 43–44
    see also Firefly
South African army, 6th Armoured
    Division **E2** (30, 31)

Tank Destroyer (US) 6–8
Tiger II tank (German) 30
Tiger VI tank (German) 5, 37, 47
track design **11**, **37**
track links, as armour protection **A1** (6)
transporters:
    Landing Craft Tank Mark 5 (LCT[5])
      32–33
    Scammell TRMU/30 **D** (26–27)
traverse gear, hydraulic and electronic
    25–26

weapons:
    bomb thrower 21
    guns
      6-pounder 5, 6
      17-pounder 5–9, 13, **18**, 28, 32,
        G1 (38), 41–42, **42**, 43–44
      Mark IV ('SH-SH' gun) 16, 17, **17**
      Mark VII (delayed action breech) 40
    ammunition 16, 18–20, **18**, 28–30
    Browning .30-in. machine gun **18**, 21
    smoke dischargers 21
    tulip rockets **A2** (6), 32
    Typhoon rockets 29
Witheridge, Maj George 9–10, 11–12